MAINE: A View from Above

MAINE
A View from Above

CHARLES FEIL

Down East Books Camden, Maine

Copyright © 1996 by Charles William Feil III
ISBN 0-89272-381-5
Book design by Janet Patterson
Color separations, printing, and binding by Regent Publishing Services
Printed in Hong Kong

1   3   5   4   2

Down East Books / Camden, Maine

LIBRARY OF CONGRESS CATALOGING-IN-PUBLICATION DATA

Feil, Charles, 1948-
    Maine : a view from above / Charles Feil.
        p.   cm.
    ISBN 0-89272-381-5
    1. Maine--Aerial photographs. I. Title.
F20. F45   1996
917.41'0022'2--dc20   96-24516
                                                            CIP

In a still-life drawing

class during my first year at the Portland School of Art (now the Maine College of Art), I was presented for the first time with an idea that struck me as being at once wildly revolutionary and utterly self-evident.

The lesson was pretty simple: henceforth we were to spend 90 percent of our time studying the object to be drawn and 10 percent of our time actually drawing it. This was, of course, the precise opposite of our youthful tendency to labor mightily over a drawing while only occasionally glancing up at the actual still life we were attempting to portray.

Thus I was introduced to the fantastic notion that the more you look at something, the more you see. I had just been handed a key capable of unlocking countless doors. If you don t believe me, here s a book that illustrates the point far more eloquently than I can explain it.

In this beautiful collection of Charles Feil s aerial photographs we not only see more of the Maine we already know and love, we are introduced to another Maine, which by some weird alchemy occupies the same time and space. In the textures, planes, and surface details there is the instant familiarity of an old friend. In the fresh angle of perspective there is the first blush of new love. Feil takes us on a guided tour of a hauntingly familiar place that we d swear we ve never seen.

In truth, this is a view of Maine that, until now, only Charles Feil has seen. I was born in the potato country of northern Aroostook County and grew up in Boothbay Harbor, idolizing fishermen and shipbuilders and forming a lifelong attachment to the ragged granite geography of the Maine coast. In the course of my career as a humorist and regular contributor to *CBS Sunday Morning* I have crisscrossed the

Mount Kineo's striking appearance is due to the sheer flint cliffs of its eastern face.

state almost continuously for the better part of three decades. I've watched the sunrise on Matinicus Island, swatted black flies in Moxie Gore Plantation, and filmed television segments in T-6/R-19. Be that as it may, Charles Feil has seen a Maine that I have not, and I'm convinced that there's more to it than having a camera and an airplane.

From the very beginning it seems that we humans have yearned to fly. We've not, however, been dreaming for centuries of sitting in a cramped metal tube sharing stale air with a piece of rubber chicken, a pulp novel, and a salesman from Cleveland. The longing of the human spirit has been to soar and dip and dive, to search out the landscape for familiar points of reference, to leap into the air and land again with the effortless grace of a swallow. It is obvious from his work that that is just the sort of flying Charles Feil does. His perspective is that of the barnstormer. His images are infused with the joy of flying as well as the joy of seeing.

And, of course, the more you look the more you see. Have you ever stopped for lunch in this town? Have you seen this church steeple bathed in the early morning sun? Observed this ice-covered river? Seen this mountain? Or watched *any* baseball game from this perspective? Whether you've seen these places before or not, you have never seen them as they are presented here. I hope you enjoy this book as much as I have. But, whatever else you do, *don't* leave it sitting on top of your coffee table. I recommend that you take a moment every now and then to pick it up, fasten your seat belt, prepare for takeoff, and enjoy the view.

—Tim Sample

Morning fog engulfs the crest of Farwell Mountain between Bethel and Newry.

The scent of morning

drifts through my bedroom window and awakens me from sleep. It is
one of those late-summer mornings in Maine where the sky is a deep
azure with warm orange tones already hinting of the coming sunrise.
I waste little time leaving my bed, for these magical mornings are my
photo opportunities. I peer out the window as I pull on my clothes,
thinking, "I've got to catch the sun cresting over Portland." Down-
stairs I grab the ever-present flight bag and backpack full of camera
gear and head out the door.

During the ten-minute drive to the airport, I think shooting
strategy: "Go south along the coast and catch the early-morning
yachtsman heading out of Kennebunkport, or more northeast toward
Boothbay Harbor and Muscongus Bay for its rugged coastline beauty?
No, I think today I'll go west toward Bethel and the mountains; it
looks like a good morning for mist rising off the lakes." I drive up to
the General Aviation parking lot, collect my gear, and head to greet the
bird that gives me wings and allows me to break the gravitational
chains of earth.

Glistening in the early rays of sunlight, my white-winged plane
seems as excited as I about breaking those chains. I walk around her
doing my preflight, touching her aluminum skin, connecting with what
will soon lift me skyward.

I climb into the cockpit and strap my backpack full of camera
gear into the right-hand seat. Attaching a 180mm lens to one camera
body and a 35–105mm zoom lens on another, I check to see that the
film is loaded and the motor drives are working properly.

Donning a headset, I begin the preflight checklist. Some 20 items
later, the Continental engine and its 285 horses fire into life. I check my

radios for the local conditions at Portland, set my instruments, and call Clearance. At the run-up area, I perform all of the final tasks before calling the tower. The moment has finally arrived for those bright wings to lift me free of the ground. I advance the throttle and begin my takeoff roll down the runway. The Continental's six cylinders roar to life, and soon the airspeed indicator comes alive. When the critical moment arrives, I pull back on the yoke. Suddenly, like a horse leaping, we slip the chains of earth and fly! With the airplane trimmed up and reaching my cruising altitude, I slow down to begin what I came up here to do: photograph the magnificent moods, contours, and colors that make up the canvas of this truly beautiful state.

The morning is much as I anticipated—calm wind, warm sun, and cool land—the ideal recipe for a carpet of low, thin ground fog in the valleys and over the lakes. I open the window of the airplane, grab the camera with the telephoto lens, and point at a hillside of pines reaching for the sun through the lacy fingers of mist. The airplane, the camera, and I create this dance for hours until the sun warms the land and it's time to head for home and the photo lab. It is on the light table that these captured moments come back to life and give meaning to the morning's experiences.

This is how it goes: spending hours in the air, always vigilant for the light, the location, the seasonal details that please the eye and make the view from above so fascinating. It is my hope that these photographs will convey a little bit of what it is like to soar above the great state of Maine.

Enjoy.

—Charles Feil

Kittery, the first town in southern Maine, is home to the Portsmouth Naval Shipyard on Seavey Island.
Here Route 1 crosses the Piscataqua River from Portsmouth, New Hampshire.

Summertime, and the living is easy in Vacationland... until it's time to leave and face the backup at the York toll booth at the southern end of the Maine Turnpike.

Ogunquit Beach, a favorite resort of Mainers and visitors alike.

My eleven-year-old son, Dylan, pointed out this shot as we flew over the Webhannet Marsh area: "I was sitting next to my dad in his plane, and out of the corner of my eye I saw this boat swerving through a canal. I poked my dad and pointed at it. I didn't think it would be that great, but it turned out very nicely, and he thought so, too."

The mouth of the Mousam River, just south of Kennebunk Beach.

Recreational and working watercraft mingle like ducks on parade at the mouth of the Kennebunk River.

On one of my many flights over Kennebunkport, I found this to be a particularly interesting composition. I call it "Three Boats on a Point."

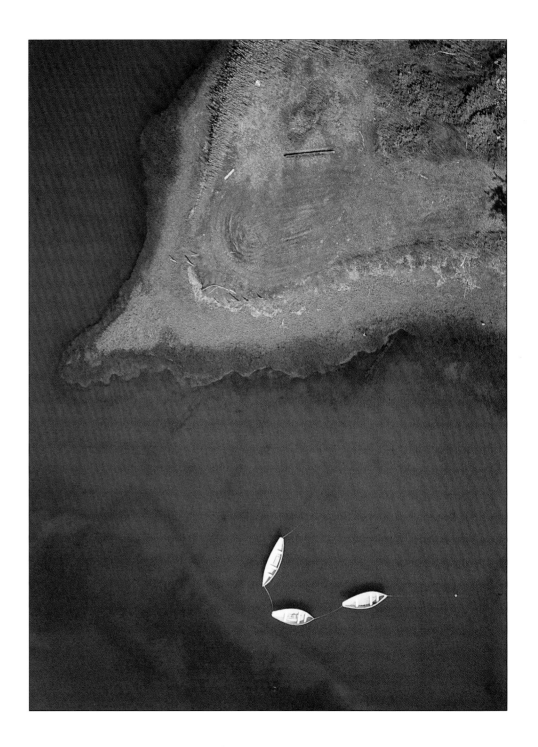

Maine's long, island-studded coast is ideal for sea kayaking. I worked my airplane into a tight circle and captured these two kayakers paddling over Goose Neck Rocks, located between Cape Porpoise and Fortunes Rocks.

Old Orchard Beach, famous for its carnival-like atmosphere and miles of fine sand beaches.

On my way back to Portland after a cold day of photographing, I dug out my camera one more time for this February sunset over Casco Bay.

Portland Head Light, off of Cape Elizabeth, is certainly one of the most photographed lighthouses in the world.
I have photographed it in all of the seasons and from every angle possible. Out of hundreds of shots, I chose this one,
taken shortly after a particularly strong summer storm that created enormous waves along the Maine coastline.

Spurwink Church, in Cape Elizabeth, is one of the oldest nondenominational churches in the state.
This photograph was made late in the summer.

Maine waters are peppered with rock shoals, a distinct hazard to boaters gunkholing along the coast. This particular shoal awaits the unwary in Casco Bay.

Cruising at five hundred feet, I caught these seagulls taking a late-afternoon spring bath in a pond on the Down East side of Peaks Island.

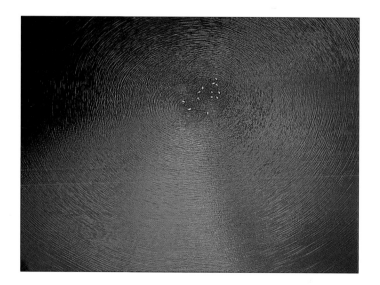

A lobsterman displays his working paraphernalia on the lawn of his Great Chebeague Island home.

Maine's largest city is also its most ethnically diverse. This view of Munjoy Hill—Portland's Little Italy—clearly shows the integration of neighborhood and the downtown business district.

Opening day at Hadlock Field, home to the Portland Sea Dogs, and the way baseball was meant to be celebrated.

DiMillo's Floating Restaurant and Marina has been a landmark of the Portland waterfront for decades.

In the summer of '95, the Maine coast was hit with a fierce coastal northeaster that produced huge swells. Spectators spent the next few evenings watching the waves crashing on the rocky coast. I spent my time in the air photographing the event. "Storm Surge Over Ram Island Ledge Light" was the result.

Build it, and they might not use it. Fort Gorges, on Hog Island ledge in Portland Harbor, was begun in 1858 but was outdated by the end of the Civil War due to the invention of cannons capable of destroying granite forts.

A hot-air balloon drifts over the Yarmouth countryside.

As much as we enjoy our summers in Maine, fall is the time for reflection and preparation for our long winters. Nature helps us to adapt by providing a bountiful array of color, as in this hardwood forest near Gorham.

Wood harvesting is one of Maine's largest industries. This clear-cut area near Steep Falls was visually interesting because of the pattern of tracks and the lighting of the few trees spared to help control erosion.

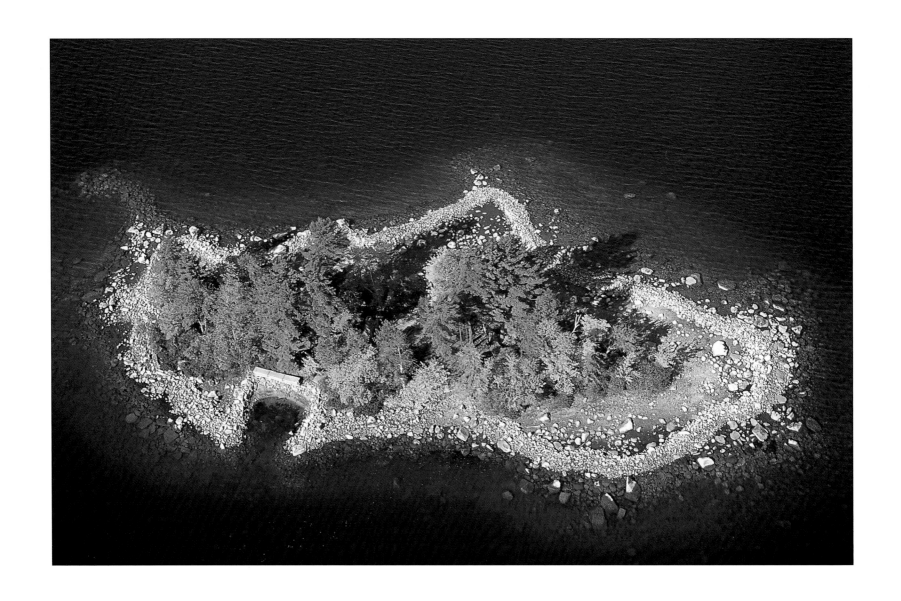

"**Paradise** (par´a dis´) *n.* [[<Gr paradeisos, garden]] 1 [P-] the garden of Eden. 2 heaven. 3 any place or state of great happiness." The Dingley Islands of Sebago Lake would easily qualify as paradise according to Mr. Webster.

A southern lake in early spring.

Twisted and aged — old tree stumps tell of a time when this wetland near Sebago Lake was drier ground.

The town of Naples is the heart and soul of the southern lakes region. With Long Lake to the west and Sebago to the east, lake enthusiasts find many recreational opportunities here.

Little Falls on the Presumpscot River frames the community of South Windham on a fall morning.

Like a Japanese print, the mountains of western Maine and New Hampshire are etched in the background of a winter sunset.

Once the power source for local industry, the mighty Androscoggin River both links and separates the sister towns of Brunswick and Topsham.

Gun Point and Hen Island stretch their glacially carved fingers out into Casco Bay.

The campus of Bowdoin College in Brunswick.

Sinuous oxbows and brackish pools
punctuate a wetland in Popham Beach
State Park.

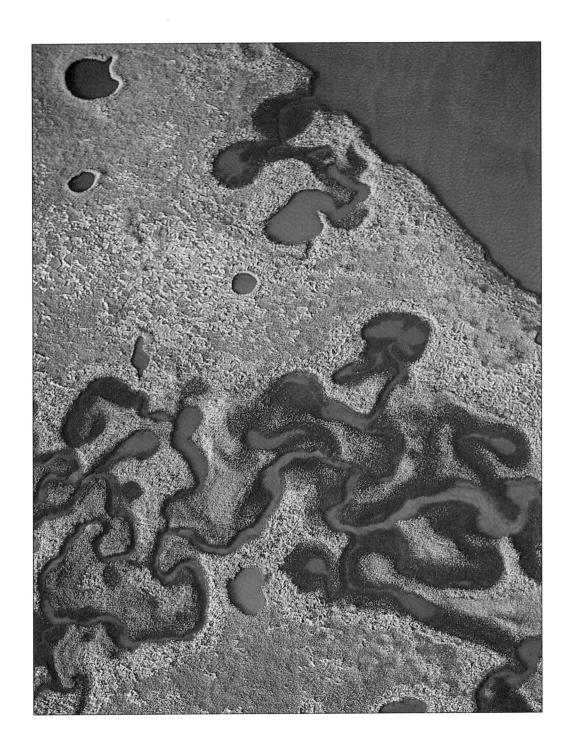

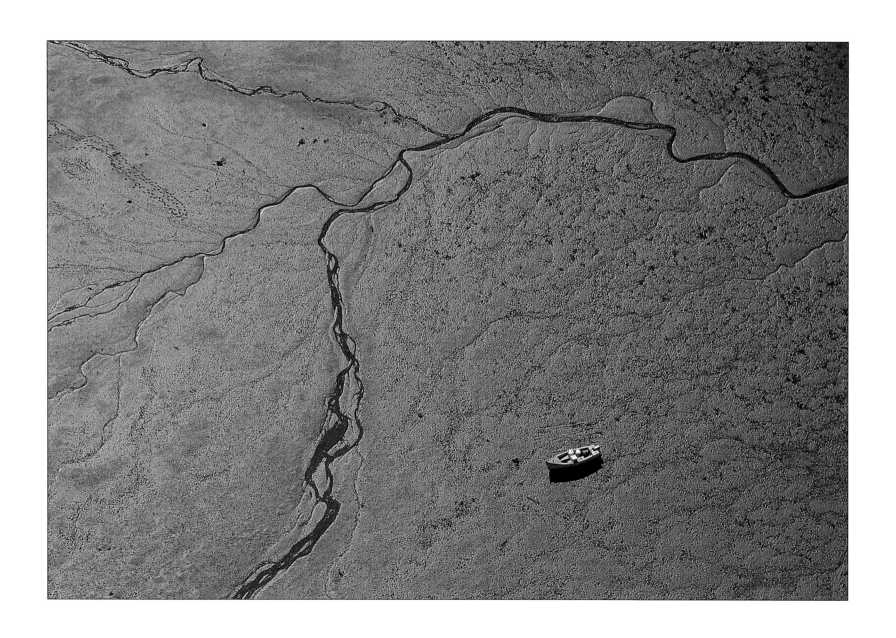

Low tide at Atkins Bay, adjacent to Popham Beach State Park.

Construction of Fort Popham began in 1861, but the semicircular granite structure was never completed. This was also the site of the Popham Colony, the first attempted English settlement on the northeast coast.

A midwinter sunset over Popham Beach.

Morning sun highlights the geometry of a mobile home park near Cook's Corner, in Bath.

Wind and ice form fascinating mosaics on the Kennebec River.

Standing 400 feet high when fully raised, the massive shipways crane at Bath Iron Works is one of the most distinctive sights in the mid-coast region.

A shadow river of mist hovers above the Eastern River in Bowdoinham.

Early one fall morning I went skyward in search of color and mist. I composed this shot over Green Point, where the Kennebec and Eastern Rivers converge.

The warm late-summer waters of lakes and rivers support huge growths of algae, such as this bloom on the Androscoggin River north of Lewiston.

Late afternoon light nicely contrasts the stately church steeples and humble homes surrounding downtown Lewiston.

Carnivals, festivals, and country fairs are a big attraction come summer's end. The Great Falls Balloon Festival, held in early September on the Auburn side of the twin cities, is one of those events.

Snow determines which ski area opens first. The eagerly awaited product of Sunday River's snowflake factory is evident in this mid-November shot.

Tendrils of mist rise off the Androscoggin River near Bethel.

Winter at Boise Cascade's Rumford paper mill.

This aeration basin is part of the water treatment system at Boise Cascade's Rumford facility.

The town of Rangeley, with Haley Pond on the left and Town Cove on the right.

Clearcuts pattern mountain flanks in the Eustis wilderness area.

I was south of Monmouth and returning to Portland when I saw this beautiful winter scene of an orchard at sunset/moonrise time.

One summer day I had decided to cruise along the Kennebec River from Moosehead Lake to where it kisses the ocean at Popham Beach. This sweet little cornfield was photographed south of Solon.

Photographing, flying, and then accurately remembering the places you've been can be overwhelming. My modus operandi has been to take my film in for processing that evening and then caption the slides the next day by mentally retracing my flight and referring to *The Maine Atlas and Gazetteer.* This works 99 percent of the time, but then there's that one percent that defy precise identification. This shot of a lovely small town somewhere in the middle of the state is one example.

The hilltop campus of Colby College, Waterville.

Kents Hill Preparatory School, between Readfield and Fayette and just up the hill from Valhalla, our summer home on Lovejoy Pond, where the trees grow tall and the loons serenade us all night long.

Maine's stately capitol building stands not far from the banks of the Kennebec River in Augusta.

Those who prefer the remote regions of Maine will often take to the skies in a floatplane like this one on Threemile Pond in the China–Windsor area.

Schooner Days, a festival of tall ships celebrated each year in Boothbay Harbor.

"Lobster Boat Amongst the Ice Floes." Outer Pemaquid Harbor.

The two schooners decaying on the banks of the Sheepscot River in Wiscasset have long been local landmarks and poignant reminders of Maine's shipbuilding heritage.

Sometimes I don't have time to plan a shot. I just grab my camera and point it out the window and shoot. This church cemetery near Waldoboro sparked one of those decisive moments.

Harbor and Hall Islands, Muscongus Bay. A favorite refuge for sailors to find a sheltered anchorage and spend a day hiking around the islands' forests and rocks.

Remote Monhegan Island is renowned as an artists' haven. Manana Island, in the foreground, flanks Monhegan Harbor.

A fishing boat and her dories filled with nets was photographed off the Rockland shore.

Carver's Harbor, on Vinalhaven Island in West Penobscot Bay.

Curtis Island invites sailors into the harbor and town of Camden.

In the nineteenth century, Rockport Harbor was dominated by smoking lime kilns. Today the now peaceful village is home to the famed Maine Photographic Workshops.

Tall ships await their morning crew and guests in Camden Harbor for a sail on Penobscot Bay.

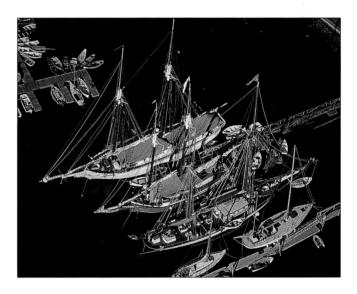

Granite quarrying continues—on a small scale—on Crotch Island, south of Stonington.

Maine's blueberry barrens are spectacular in the fall. These are near Blue Hill.

This majestic span across Eggemoggin Reach connects the Blue Hill area with Little Deer Isle.

Stonington, an active fishing village on the tip of Deer Isle, overlooks a vast and beautiful archipelago that includes rugged Isle au Haut. Much of the town is perched on the steep ledges of an old granite quarry.

Sea-swept smooth ledges outline Potato Island in the Isle au Haut archipelago.

Fort Knox, in Prospect, doesn't protect any gold;
it was built (between 1846 and 1865) to defend
the Penobscot River valley should Britain try to
renew its old claims to eastern Maine lands.
It is the only Maine fort with some of its original
cannons still emplaced.

This little gem of a church overlooks Penobscot
Bay from a hillside on Isle au Haut.

The Penobscot River was once the economic lifeblood of Bangor, Maine's second-largest city.

New-growth forest in a clearcut site, Somerset County.

Greenville, the end of the road (unless you're heading west) and the site to launch your boat or seaplane and explore the Moosehead Lake region.

Sandbar Island unfolds itself across Moosehead Lake.

An early snowfall clearly delineates the Knife Edge of Katahdin, Maine's highest and most rugged peak.

Skidder tracks superimpose a manmade uniformity on the Allagash wilderness.

These logs are destined for the Georgia-Pacific mill in Woodland, where they will be turned into pulp and processed into paper.

Potato harvesting near Houlton.

Harvested potato fields, Frenchville region.

The St. John River snakes between the borders of Maine and Canada. Fort Kent stands as one of Maine's northernmost outposts.

Late fall woodland near Caribou.

The serene potato farming community of St. Agatha, on Long Lake.

Glaciers sculpted the formation known as Dung Fork Points in Baskahegan Lake.

If you were to travel all the way up the East Coast from Key West, Lubec would be the last U.S. town you would pass through before entering Canada.

The huge array of antennas at North Cutler is used to contact American submarines in the North Atlantic.

Aquaculture is changing the face of the fishing industry in towns like Jonesport.

It looks like a Bahamian beach, but it is our very own pristine oasis — Roque Island, north of Jonesport.

A century apart. The starkly new structure on Jordan's Delight faces 140-year-old Narraguagus Light on Pond Island.

Petit Manan Light was erected in 1817. At 119 feet, its tower is the second highest in Maine.

Northeast Harbor on Mt. Desert Island. The Hadlock Ponds are in the background.

The noble stone bridge across Duck Brook is a gateway to the town of Bar Harbor.

Cadillac Mountain is the highest point on the eastern seaboard, and one of the most trekked upon, though you wouldn't know it at six o'clock on a fall morning.

In life and in art,

the shortest distance between two points can be very dull. This is true whether you're flying a plane or scouting for a good camera shot—and especially if you're doing both at the same time. My path between photography and flying spanned some twenty years before finally making the connection, not exactly the shortest or dullest route.

In the mid-'60s, while still in my teens, I joined VISTA (domestic Peace Corps) and set off for New Mexico. I lived in a barrio in Albuquerque and became involved in community development, working with Mexican-American boys not much younger than myself. I soon felt that I needed to record this experience somehow. A friend offered to lend me a camera—and donate a roll of film—provided I learn the mysteries of the darkroom as well. I accepted the challenge.

When the first shadows of an image began to rise on the paper in the tray of developer, I knew I had discovered my true destiny. I now took a camera with me everywhere. Magazines and newspapers bought my work. I went to Africa three times on assignment. But when I saw that most of my work was being done for corporations and for advertising, I felt I needed to change things. I moved to Maine and moved in with my lifetime mate, and together we started an outerwear clothing design business.

It became a time of new adventures, romance, imagination, and opportunities for new freedoms. In January 1992, a friend asked to borrow a set of strobe lights from me. He was a flight instructor and offered to trade a few hours of flight training in exchange for the use of the lights. I accepted. It would be another challenge—a spontaneous exit from my earthbound responsibilities.

Immediately I had visions of marrying my photographic talent to my newfound love of flight. By the winter of '92 I had attained my instrument rating, and confidence in my flying abilities grew after I completed training for a commercial license a year later. I flew the plane accompanied by a safety pilot and began seriously taking photos of the Maine countryside. I soon realized that I was a pretty heavy renter of the Cessna 172 I was flying and decided that it might be an appropriate time to invest in an airplane and set it up for my particular style of making photographs.

I prefer to pilot and set up my photos with as few encumbrances as possible, so I don't use any gyros or special filters (other than the one to protect the lens). My technique requires just my instincts, an open window, a Nikon 35mm camera and a couple of good lenses, Fujichrome film, and quick visual editing of an immense subject. My photographs are intended to be my own unique, spontaneous impressions of a landscape of unparalleled beauty and challenge.